every teenager's
little black book
on cool

by blaine bartel

every teenager's
little black book
on cool

by blaine bartel

Harrison House
Tulsa, Oklahoma

Unless otherwise indicated, all Scripture quotations are taken from
the *King James Version* of the Bible.

Scripture quotations marked NKJV are taken from *The New King James
Version*. Copyright © 1979, 1980, 1982, Thomas Nelson, Inc.

06 05 04   10 9 8 7 6 5

Every Teenager's Little Black Book on Cool
ISBN 1-57794-459-3
Copyright © 2002 by Blaine Bartel
P.O. Box 691923
Tulsa, Oklahoma 74179

Published by Harrison House, Inc.
P.O. Box 35035
Tulsa, Oklahoma 74153

contents

contents (continued)

Finding Favor

Design a Cool Future

contents (continued)

Cool, Hard Cash

The Unselfish Life

[COOL DOESN'T TRY]

3 REASONS WHY COOL DOESN'T TRY—IT IS

Truly cool people don't have to work at it—they just are. Let's be honest: if you have to try to be cool, you probably won't have a lot of people looking up to you. Let's check out 3 reasons why cool doesn't have to try.

1. **Being cool is an honor that only others can bestow upon you.** Remember, the Bible's counterparts for the modern word *cool* are *favored* and *accepted*. Only God and people can show you favor and acceptance.

2. **Truly cool people focus on others, not on themselves.** Matthew 23:12 says that those who humble themselves will be exalted.

3. **Most cool people don't even realize they are cool.** They're too busy making a difference in their world.

4 THINGS THAT ARE DEFINITELY NOT COOL

Have you ever had someone at school try to impress you in some way? They were thinking, *Wow! Am I ever cool!* And you were thinking, *When is this person going to get a clue?* Once again, cool people don't have to work to impress you. Here are 4 things that are definitely not cool.

1. You are not cool when you talk about yourself most of the time. The Bible says, "Let another man praise you, and not your own mouth" (Prov. 27:2 NKJV).

2. You are not cool because of how you walk or what you wear. You are accepted and favored because of the good person you are, not the perception you try to create.

3. It is definitely not cool to live a life of sin and personal pleasure. The Word of God warns us, "The way of transgressors is hard" (Prov. 13:15).

4. It is not cool to make others feel small by putting them down with your words. Remember the law of

sowing and reaping—if you sow encouragement, you'll reap it back.

5 WAYS TO KNOW YOU AREN'T COOL

Maybe you're reading this little book right now and you're still not sure: *Am I cool?* So I want to help you with some important identification marks of people who will not gain favor with others. Here are 5 ways to know you aren't cool.

1. If you constantly live in self-pity, looking to get attention, you are not cool.

2. If you try to impress people with your money, possessions, or accomplishments, you are not cool.

3. If you are sharp-tongued, gossipy, and critical of others, you are not cool.

4. If you only treat people you like and know with love and respect, you are not cool.

5. If you spend the majority of the time thinking about yourself, having little regard for Christ and others, you are not cool.

4 REASONS YOU SHOULD BE COOL

God wants you to be cool, accepted, and favored. The Scripture says, "Let not mercy and truth forsake you; bind them around your neck, write them on the tablet of your heart, and so find favor and high esteem in the sight of God and man" (Prov. 3:3,4 NKJV). You can enjoy favor, acceptance, and popularity with both God and people. Here are 4 reasons why you should be cool.

1. Cool, accepted people have the ability to influence others for good. That includes a witness of your Christian faith.

2. Cool, favored people have confidence to do things others believe to be impossible or improbable.

3. Accepted people find it easy and natural to show others God's love and acceptance.

4. Cool people stand up for truth and don't need everyone to agree with them or even like them.

6 WAYS ANY PERSON CAN BECOME COOL

Let's get right to the point: you want to be accepted and popular with people. Who doesn't? Now, you know you can't try to gain popularity and "coolness" the way the world tries to manufacture it. So how does a person become "Christ-like cool"?

1. You become cool when you stand up for what is right and don't care who stands with you.

2. You become cool when you reach out to the poor, the hurting, the lost—those who are "uncool."

3. You become cool when you take time for those whom many overlook—children. God loves kids, and so should we.

4. You become cool when you freely admit your short-comings, pick up where you've failed, and move forward with godly confidence.

5. You become cool when you put God first in your words, your actions, and your plans.

6. You become cool when you could care less about being cool.

[COOL CONFIDENCE]

4 DIFFERENCES BETWEEN
CONFIDENCE AND ARROGANCE

Some people think that confidence is pride. You can be confident and very humble. Pride is confidence in the wrong things. True confidence comes from a solid foundation of knowing who you are in Christ. Look at these 4 differences between confidence and arrogance and check up on yourself.

1. Confidence is security in who we are in Christ. Arrogance is self-reliance because of what we have, who we know, or what we have done.

2. Confidence is knowing that "we can do all things through Christ Jesus" versus trusting what we can do ourselves. (Phil. 4:13.)

3. Confidence is knowing our past is forgiven by God and we are in good standing with Him by faith. Arrogance is confidence in our works and our righteousness. (Eph. 2:8.)

4. Confidence is knowing that God is on our side and, therefore, it doesn't matter who is against us.

Arrogance is security from circumstances and our own resources. (Rom. 8:31.)

Be confident because of who you are in Christ Jesus. With Him on your side, you can't fail.

5 MARKS OF A CONFIDENT PERSON

Use this as a check to see if you are confident in who you arc in Christ.

1. You aren't afraid to meet new people.

2. You like to try new things and see new places.

3. You aren't afraid to take calculated risks in order to achieve something you want.

4. You don't get discouraged and depressed when you fail. Instead, you pick yourself back up.

5. It doesn't bother you much when people criticize you.

If all of the statements above describe you, you are very confident. If 4 of the statements are true about you, your confidence is solid and improving. Three true statements means you could use some improvement. It's not looking good if only 2 statements are true; you are limiting yourself from great experiences. If you only found 1 statement to be true,

reread this book every day until all the statements are true.
Remember, in Christ you are a new creation. (2 Cor. 5:17.)

3 MUSTS FOR BUILDING REAL CONFIDENCE

If you need more confidence in your life, here is a simple game plan that will help you grow.

1. **Find your identity in Christ Jesus.** If we look to ourselves for confidence, we have many reasons to be insecure and disappointed. But in Christ, we are amazing. Look up these Scriptures: 2 Corinthians 5:17; Philippians 4:13; Colossians 1:22; Jude 24; Romans 8:15.

2. **Surround yourself with people who believe in you.** Small people criticize big dreams. Don't allow your faith and self-esteem to be robbed by critical and negative people. Surround yourself with people who believe in you.

3. **Take small steps to build big victories.** We all have things in our lives we are secretly afraid of. Maybe it's heights, meeting new people, trying new foods, or sharing our faith. Don't take a leap of faith; take little steps toward overcoming your fears. The

Bible says, "The steps of a good man are ordered by the Lord" (Ps. 37:23).

Build these 3 steps to confidence into your daily routine, and watch your confidence soar.

6 ENEMIES THAT WILL TRY
TO STEAL YOUR CONFIDENCE

In battle, one of the best advantages you can have is to understand your enemy. The more you know your enemy, the better you can avoid his traps and attacks. Here are 6 enemies that will try to steal your confidence.

1. **Negative people who criticize you.** You get to choose who your friends are. If your friends pull you down, get new friends.

2. **Unconfessed sin.** This will rob your confidence before God. Don't be like Adam and Eve who hid from God. Go to Him, confess it, and be forgiven. (1 John 1:9.)

3. **Listening to your feelings rather than God's Word.** Feelings will betray you because they are subject to your circumstances. Fix your eyes on God's unchanging Word.

4. **Looking at your past to determine your future.** You may have a past littered with failure, but that

doesn't mean you can't succeed. A righteous person falls 7 times but keeps getting back up. (Prov. 24:16.)

5. **Looking at the problem rather than God's promise for the solution.** God's Word has a promise for any problem you face.

6. **Comparing yourself to other people.** You are a great you but a lousy anyone else. Be you. You are great. (Jer. 1:5, 29:11; Ps. 138:8, 139.)

Don't let the enemy steal your confidence. You have every reason to be secure. You're on God's team, and we win.

7 SCRIPTURES THAT PROVE GOD IS CONFIDENT IN YOU

Here are 7 encouraging Scriptures to look up and commit to memory.

1. **Psalm 138:8:** God will fulfill His purpose for your life.

2. **John 3:16:** God believed in you enough to allow His Son, Jesus, to die for you.

3. **Mark 16:15:** After Jesus rose from the dead, He gave His ministry to His disciples and us to finish.

4. **Jude 24:** He said He will keep you from falling and present you in His presence with great joy.

5. **Acts 1:8:** He gave us His power and Holy Spirit to witness.

6. **John 15:16:** He handpicked you. You're His first-round draft pick.

7. **Ephesians 2:5:** Even while we were lost, He made us alive with Him.

If God is confident in you, that should be enough for you. He is the Creator of the universe, and He is on your side. You can't lose.

[FINDING FAVOR]

4 STEPS TO FINDING FAVOR WITH GOD

Let's be honest. If you can get yourself in favor with the most powerful Person in the universe, you're going to do really well. The great thing is that God has told us clearly in His Word that we can fall into favor with Him. Here are 5 steps to getting there.

1. **Diligently seek after Him.** He promises to reward and bless anyone who wholeheartedly seeks Him. (Heb. 11:6.)

2. **Search out the wisdom of God's Word.** He promises that when we discover His wisdom we will obtain favor from Him. (Prov. 8:35.)

3. **Develop a lifestyle of praising God without apology.** The churches in the book of Acts were bold to praise God with their voices and found favor with all the people. (Acts 2:47.)

4. **Walk into goodness and integrity towards others.** God promises you favor, but condemns the person who is wicked in one's actions. (Prov. 12:2.)

4 STEPS TO FINDING FAVOR WITH FRIENDS

Everyone wants to have good friends. In order to have a good friend, you must learn to be one. There are very real reasons why everyone seems to like some people, while others are constantly rejected. Here are 4 practical steps to finding good friends.

1. **Break out of your shell of fear.** Don't wait for people to reach out to you. Be bold to say hello to people and make conversation.

2. **Give friends their space.** Don't monopolize people's time or constantly follow them around. When you begin to smother people with attention, they will naturally want to avoid you.

3. **Be confident in yourself and your abilities.** If you are constantly putting yourself down and wallowing in self-pity, people will tire of you soon.

4. **Have a giving heart without trying to "buy" your friendships.** Be generous and thoughtful

without feeling like you have to do things to keep a certain friend. If you have to buy or give someone something all the time, the person is probably not a friend anyway.

3 STEPS TO FINDING FAVOR
WITH THE OPPOSITE SEX

There is something that happens when you move into your teenage years. All of a sudden, you're not as concerned about "girls' germs" or "boys' germs" as you were when you were 7 or 8. During your teens, God slowly prepares you to someday enter into the covenant of marriage. It is important that you learn how to properly treat and respect the opposite sex, since you will eventually live with one of them forever. Here are 3 simple steps to remember.

1. **Learn how to pass on sincere compliments about their character and accomplishments.** Make them feel appreciated for who they are and what they've worked hard to achieve.

2. **Be nice to all.** Don't become "a snob" or "stuck up" because you only associate with those who are good-looking or popular. Remember, Jesus died and shed His blood for every person, not just the ones He liked.

3. **Show respect and purity physically.** Your body belongs to you. Other people's bodies belong to them.

The only time this changes is when 2 people are married. So, until that time comes for you, stay clear of tempting situations. (1 Cor. 7:1-4.)

6 STEPS TO FINDING FAVOR
IN THE WORKPLACE

God wants to help you succeed in all your work. Your success in your job and career will be a direct result of your ability to get along with people. One of the coolest things in the world is having a job you love and working with people you really like. Here are 6 steps to get you there.

1. Don't treat your boss one way and everyone else a different way. People will see your hypocrisy and resent you.

2. Never cheat your company or business by stealing. I'm not just talking about their products or supplies; this also includes their time. If you're constantly late to work, taking long breaks, or leaving early, it's like stealing money out of the cash register, because "Time is money."

3. Don't try to destroy someone at your work in order to get that person's position for yourself. It will eventually backfire, and you'll be out!

4. When someone else does a good job at your work, compliment the person personally and in front of your boss.

5. Never try to take authority or leadership that hasn't been given to you. Just do your job, and stay out of business that isn't yours.

6. Always give 100 percent. If you can give 110 percent, you were never giving 100 percent in the first place!

3 STEPS TO FINDING FAVOR
WITH YOUR PARENTS

One of the coolest things in life is enjoying a happy home. You can learn to become a source of joy in your family. I've got 3 teenage boys who everyone at school and church thinks are really "cool." But they are also great guys at home. The rebel attitude is not cool. In fact, it will cause you some very "uncool" moments in life. Here are 3 things you can do to ensure a great time at home.

1. **Choose to obey your parents immediately, whether you feel like it or not.** You're eventually going to have to do it—right? So just get it done and out of the way.

2. **Honor your parents when you speak to them.** Even if you don't agree with them and want to discuss something or negotiate a "better deal," do it without the anger and the attitude. You'll be amazed at the results!

3. **Be truthful, even when it gets you in trouble.**

You lose favor quickly when you cannot be trusted. It is better to take the heat if you have it coming, than to lie and avoid it. Lies are eventually uncovered, and the consequences are much more damaging than telling the truth would have been.

[DESIGN A

COOL FUTURE]

7 ABSOLUTES OF GOD'S WILL FOR YOUR LIFE

Have you ever heard someone say, "God moves in mysterious ways"? I sure am glad that statement isn't true. The will of God doesn't have to be mysterious. Here are 7 things you can absolutely count on.

1. **God's will is salvation.** Our heavenly Father desires that all of humankind have eternal life with Him. That includes you.

2. **God's will is dominion.** Dominion simply means control. God wants you to apply His Word and take control of your body, thought life, attitude, and future.

3. **God's will is discipleship.** We are to grow in our walk with Christ. As we mature, we are to help others do the same.

4. **God's will is unity.** Your words and actions must be united with God's Word.

5. **God's will is stewardship.** We are to take proper care of our time, money, abilities, and all God has entrusted us with.

6. **God's will is relationships.** Through the power of relationships, you will be able to accomplish things that would be impossible if you were alone.

7. **God's will is progressive.** God has a plan for your life that will be completed one step at a time, not in leaps or bounds.

4 WAYS GOD GIVES YOU DIRECTION

Do you need direction? Good, because God wants to give it to you. The direction of God is not hard to come by. Here are 4 ways He will give it to you.

1. **The Word (Bible):** the most practical way that God gives direction. All other ways must line up with this way.

2. **Peace:** how God will lead you. His peace will be deep down inside letting you know you're headed in the right direction.

3. **People:** pastors, teachers, parents, and friends. God will speak through these people whom He has strategically placed in your life.

4. **Desires:** what you want to do. Do you like making art, building, or helping others? God has placed desires in your heart to help give you direction.

5 DECISIONS YOUNG PEOPLE MAKE
THAT SABOTAGE THEIR FUTURE

Who you are now and who you will be is determined by the decisions you make. One out of every one person will make decisions. When you have to make a decision and don't, that is in itself a decision. So the question is what kind of decision-maker are you going to be? To help keep you from sabotaging your future, here are 5 decisions *not* to make.

1. **Disobey your parents.** God has placed your parents in your life to help guide you.

2. **Make quick decisions.** Before making a decision, take time to think it over.

3. **Develop wrong relationships.** The people you spend time with probably have the most influence on the decisions you make.

4. **Wait for your big break.** You must get off the couch and pursue your God-given destiny.

5. **Give up.** Both winners and losers face challenges, but winners don't quit.

6 STEPS TO FINDING YOUR HUSBAND OR WIFE

Finding that special person God has for you is one of the most important journeys you will take. Here are 6 steps to help you in your search.

1. **Prepare.** Be sure you are ready emotionally and, most importantly, spiritually.

2. **Ask.** Pray for guidance in finding your spouse. Remember: you have not because you ask not. (James 4:2.)

3. **Obey**. Obedience to God's Word will keep you on the right track.

4. **Focus.** Keep your eyes and heart on Jesus, not the anxiety of searching.

5. **Wait.** Be patient and understand that God has a perfect time for your paths to cross.

6. **Relax.** As you are doing your part, God will take care of the rest.

3 KEYS TO EFFECTIVE PLANNING

If you want success, you must plan for it. Someone once asked Wayne Gretzky how he became the best goal scorer in the history of hockey. He replied, "While everyone else is chasing the puck, I go to where the puck is going to be." He planned ahead. Let's take a look at 3 keys to effective planning.

1. **Prayer.** You may not know what the future holds, but God does. God promises that if you will ask Him, He will show you things that you could never figure out on your own. (Jer. 33:3.)

2. **Goal setting.** Write out exactly what it is you are planning for. You will be amazed how this key will unlock your future.

3. **Prioritizing.** You can't keep your priorities if you don't have any. Putting things in order will help you plan for and accomplish the most important things first.

[COOL, HARD CASH]

3 REASONS IT IS COOL TO MAKE GOOD MONEY

In the past, some Christians have believed and taught that all Christians should be poor. Sadly, they have had a very poor understanding of what God says in the Bible. While the Lord is opposed to us making money our god and primary focus, He wants to bring finances into our hands for the right purposes. Check out 3 reasons why making good money is cool with Him.

1. God wants you to learn how to provide well for yourself and your family. In fact, He says that if you don't make money and provide for your home, you are worse than an infidel (a really bad sinner)! (1 Tim. 5:8.)

2. God wants you to use your money to sow into His kingdom in order to make provision to take the message of Christ around the world. It costs money to print Bibles, support missionaries, and build soul-winning churches. (2 Cor. 9:6-11.)

3. Simply, God loves His children. As a Father, He wants to meet all of our needs and even our desires. As long

as we keep our eyes and hearts focused on Him, it is His will to bless us abundantly. (Ps. 37:4; Matt. 6:33; Phil. 4:19.)

5 WAYS TO GET A GREAT JOB

I've held a job since I was 12 years old. I've learned how to work hard and have never, ever been fired. I've discovered that if you give your best, you will have the opportunity to eventually do work that you enjoy and get promoted into a really cool job. Here are 5 ways to land a great job or career.

1. Get out into the workplace and hunt your job down. Knock on doors, set up interviews, and learn to sell your desire and ability.

2. Be sure you have properly trained and prepared yourself for the job you really want. If it means college, find a way to get to college. Read, learn, intern, volunteer, and do whatever it takes to become the best in your field.

3. Start out in any company or organization being willing to do the small things that other "big shots" aren't willing to do. It will separate and distinguish you from the pack.

4. Set your sights high. Don't allow your own self-doubt or other people's lack of support to stop you from going after your goals. (Mark 11:24.)

5. Pray and trust God to open up the doors supernaturally. He can, and He will. (Jer. 33:3.)

3 KINDS OF GIVING EVERY PERSON
OUGHT TO DO

One of the unbreakable laws of the universe is the law of sowing and reaping, seedtime and harvest. (Gen. 8:22.) It usually doesn't feel like it at the time, but when you give your money into the ground of good works, it will produce and come back to you multiplied many times over. Here are 5 kinds of "money-seed" you should sow, expecting God to bring a harvest back to you.

1. Sow the tithe into your local church. A tithe is one-tenth of what you earn, and we are commanded in Scripture to give into the "storehouse," or where we receive our primary spiritual food—our church. (Mal. 3:10.)

2. Sow special offerings or gifts into ministries that are reaching people and to other worthy causes that are truly impacting people. (Phil. 4:15-19.)

3. Sow into the lives of those who are poor and unable to provide for themselves. (Prov. 22:9.) Keep your gift as

private as possible so as not to humiliate the one who receives it.

4 THINGS COOL PEOPLE LEARN
TO BUY THE RIGHT WAY

In life, you are going to do a lot of spending. I believe it is important to be a good steward of the money God gives by being wise in the way we purchase things. It is completely "uncool" to waste our money on things that don't last or are unhealthy or unproductive. Now for the things you must learn to buy right.

1. **Luxuries.** This is the stuff you really don't "need" but would be cool to have. A couple of points to remember: don't make impulsive purchases; allow a cooling-off period before you pull the trigger; never put a luxury on credit—pay cash; allow luxury purchases in proper proportion to your budget for the rest of your expenses.

2. **Vehicle.** This is the big-ticket item. When starting out, don't buy a brand-new one. You'll lose a few thousand dollars the minute you drive it off the lot. Be careful as you search for a good used vehicle. Compare prices, get the vehicle checked by an

independent mechanic, and make sure you can afford the payments if you finance it.

3. **Food.** Stay away from a lot of junk. Learn to eat healthy!

4. **Clothes.** Cheap clothes are tempting, but they often don't last or look very good. Spend a little extra to get something sharp.

5. **House.** It's probably a little way down the road for you right now, but don't allow yourself to have a "renter's mentality." The quicker you can buy your own place, even if it's a "fixer-upper," the better! Get wise counsel from those who have purchased several homes successfully.

3 INVESTMENTS ANY TEENAGER SHOULD START RIGHT NOW

One of the coolest things is to see a young person who has learned early on the discipline of setting money aside for the future. Early financial investment will bring great rewards. If a parent put $1000 a year into an investment that reaps 10 percent for just the first 10 years of a child's life, when that child reached 60, there would be more than $1 million from that $1000 investment. The point is to start doing something now. Here are 3 ideas:

1. Go to your parents' bank, open a savings account, and commit to put a certain amount in it every month.

2. Save up your money to buy shares of stock in a strong American company, such as Wal-Mart, GE, and others that you know will be around a long time. Then leave it! Forget it's even there, and in about 20 or 30 years you'll be amazed at how it grows!

3. Once you get a regular job, commit to put at least 10 percent of your income each month into savings,

stocks, or mutual funds. If you need wisdom and help as to how to do this most effectively, talk to a financial counselor at your bank or someone in your church who is financially successful.

[THE UNSELFISH LIFE]

4 REASONS PEOPLE BECOME SELFISH

Have you ever wondered how someone could be so selfish?
To answer that question and to help you avoid that same
pitfall, here is a list of 4 reasons why people become selfish.

1. **They make the choice to be selfish.** We must
   make a decision not to be selfish, even if we don't feel
   like it. I have found that as you act on your decision,
   the feelings will come.

2. **They take for granted the joy of giving.** Not only
   will an unselfish act bring joy to others, but the giver
   will receive joy as well.

3. **They have unrenewed thinking.** We're all born
   naturally selfish, but that doesn't mean we must stay
   that way. We need to put selfless thoughts in and
   selfish thoughts out.

4. **They're unthankful.** Unthankfulness will cause
   people to become selfish. People who are unthankful
   stop recognizing the goodness of others; therefore,
   they develop an unwillingness to give.

5 UNSELFISH ACTS IN THE BIBLE

Do you need a role model of unselfishness? The stories of the Bible have been placed there for our example. Let's take a look at 5 unselfish acts we can imitate.

1. **Abraham and Isaac. (Gen. 22.)** Abraham was willing to give his beloved son for the cause of God.

2. **The crucifixion of Christ. (Matt. 27.)** Jesus Christ, being without sin, died the death of a criminal so that we could live a life free from sin.

3. **Joseph and his brothers. (Gen. 37-45.)** Joseph did not strike back in vengeance towards his brothers, who sold him into slavery, when he had the opportunity to do so.

4. **The poor widow. (Luke 21:1-4.)** Although poor, this widow gave all she could give.

5. **The Good Samaritan. (Luke 10:30-36.)** This Samaritan acted unselfishly, regardless of what others might have thought.

5 SCRIPTURES THAT FOCUS ON GIVING

Every day you will have a choice whether to give or not to give. Whether your little brother wants to borrow something or a crazy friend wants you to shave his back hair, here for your encouragement are 5 Scriptures on giving.

1. **Luke 6:38:** Giving not only blesses the receiver, but also the giver.

2. **Proverbs 21:26:** As the righteousness of God, we are not to be stingy in our giving.

3. **2 Corinthians 9:7:** Be sure your heart is in the right place while giving.

4. **Matthew 10:8:** God has blessed us so that we may bless others.

5. **Acts 20:35:** The giver is better off than the one who receives.

6 PRACTICAL ACTIONS OF
LOVE TOWARDS OTHERS

God is love, and as imitators of Christ we are to illuminate His love towards others. Maybe you need some advice to get started. Here are some potential actions to get the ball rolling.

1. **Be polite.** Treat others with respect. Say please and thank you. Also remember, guys: ladies first.

2. **Smile.** Show off those pearly whites. This small gesture will go a long way.

3. **Share.** This unselfish act is packed with power.

4. **Listen.** Give others your full attention. They will appreciate the investment.

5. **Lend a hand.** Mow the lawn for an elderly neighbor, or send a card to a relative you have been praying for.

6. **Give a gift.** There doesn't have to be a special reason, but the best reason of all is to simply say, "I love you."

3 REASONS GIVERS FIND UNUSUAL FAVOR

Favor can bring you before the right people and set up the right circumstances. Wouldn't you like to have favor? As a giver, you can. Here's why:

1. **It's a spiritual law.** As you give, it is as if you are making deposits into a favor bank account that you can withdraw at any time. (Luke 6:38.)

2. **People like givers.** As you give, you become a giant magnet for unusual favor. Don't you enjoy being around givers? I thought so.

3. **God is on your side.** As you are obedient to God's Word, God will open up doors of favor in your life.

MEET BLAINE BARTEL

Past: Came to Christ at age 16 on the heels of the Jesus movement. While in pursuit of a professional freestyle skiing career, answered God's call to reach young people. Developed and hosted groundbreaking television series *Fire by Nite*. Planted and pastored a growing church in Colorado Springs.

Present: Serves under his pastor and mentor of nearly 20 years, Willie George, senior pastor of 12,000-member Church on the Move in Tulsa, Oklahoma. Youth pastor of Oneighty®, America's largest local church youth ministry, and reaches more than 1,500 students weekly. National director of Oneighty's® worldwide outreaches, including a network of over 400 affiliated youth ministries. Host of Elevate, one of the largest annual youth leadership training conferences in the nation. Host of *Thrive*™, youth leader audio resource series listened to by thousands each month.

Passion: Summed up in 3 simple words: "Serving America's Future." Life quest is "to relevantly introduce the person of Jesus Christ to each new generation of young people, leaving footprints for future leaders to follow."

Personal: Still madly in love with his wife and partner of 20 years, Cathy. Raising 3 boys who love God, Jeremy—17, Dillon—15, and Brock—13. Avid hockey player and fan, with a rather impressive Gretzky memorabilia collection.

To contact Blaine Bartel,

write:

Blaine Bartel

Serving America's Future

P.O. Box 691923

Tulsa, OK 74169

www.blainebartel.com

Please include your prayer requests
and comments when you write.

To contact Oneighty®, write:

Oneighty®

P.O. Box 770

Tulsa, OK 74101

www.Oneighty.com

OTHER BOOKS BY BLAINE BARTEL

Ten Rules to Youth Ministry and Why Oneighty® Breaks Them All

every teenager's
Little Black Book
on sex and dating

every teenager's
Little Black Book
on cash

every teenager's
Little Black Book
of hard to find information

PRAYER OF SALVATION

A born-again, committed relationship with God is the key to a victorious life. Jesus, the Son of God, laid down His life and rose again so that we could spend eternity with Him in heaven and experience His absolute best on earth. The Bible says, "For God so loved the world, that he gave his only begotten Son, that whosoever believeth in him should not perish, but have everlasting life" (John 3:16).

It is the will of God that everyone receive eternal salvation. The way to receive this salvation is to call upon the name of Jesus and confess Him as your Lord. The Bible says, "That if thou shalt confess with thy mouth the Lord Jesus, and shalt believe in thine heart that God hath raised him from the dead, thou shalt be saved. For whosoever shall call upon the name of the Lord shall be saved" (Romans 10:9,13).

Jesus has given salvation, healing, and countless benefits to all who call upon His name. These benefits can be yours if you receive Him into your heart by praying this prayer:

Heavenly Father, I come to You admitting that I am a sinner. Right now, I choose to turn away

*from sin, and I ask You to cleanse me of all
unrighteousness. I believe that Your Son, Jesus,
died on the cross to take away my sins. I also
believe that He rose again from the dead so that I
may be justified and made righteous through faith
in Him. I call upon the name of Jesus Christ to be
the Savior and Lord of my life. Jesus, I choose to
follow You, and I ask that You fill me with the
power of the Holy Spirit. I declare right now that I
am a born-again child of God. I am free from sin,
and full of the righteousness of God. I am saved
in Jesus' name, amen.*

If you have prayed this prayer to receive Jesus Christ as your
Savior, or if this book has changed your life, we would like to
hear from you. Please write us at:

Harrison House Publishers

P.O. Box 35035

Tulsa, Oklahoma 74153

You can also visit us on the Web at

www.harrisonhouse.com

Additional copies of this book
are available from your local bookstore.

HARRISON HOUSE

Tulsa, Oklahoma 74153

THE HARRISON HOUSE VISION

Proclaiming the truth and the power
Of the Gospel of Jesus Christ
With excellence;

Challenging Christians to
Live victoriously,
Grow spiritually,
Know God intimately.